RABBITS

Hamlyn
PET CARE
Handbooks

RABBITS

Keith and Joyce
Lawrence

HAMLYN

Published by
The Hamlyn Publishing Group Limited
Bridge House, 69 London Road
Twickenham, Middlesex TW1 3SB, England
and distributed for them by
Octopus Distribution Services Limited
Rushden, Northamptonshire NN10 9RZ, England

First published 1987

ISBN 0 600 55142 3

Some of the material in this book
is reproduced from other books published
by The Hamlyn Publishing Group Ltd.

Printed in Hong Kong by Mandarin Offset

Contents

Introduction

All today's breeds of rabbit are derived from the wild rabbit, which originated in the Western Mediterranean region. Wild rabbits were at one time especially common in Spain and North Africa, and it is probable that the Romans started to domesticate them during the third century BC.

Some writers suggest that as a result of domestication, these rabbits produced a very hardy strain which proved adaptable and spread, or was introduced, into Northern Europe.

Wild rabbits were not reported on the English mainland until the late 12th century, towards the end of the Norman period. Indeed, one historical source suggests that they arrived during the reign of King Stephen (1135–54). For at least 400 years after their arrival the name 'rabbit' was applied only to the young, which today are called 'kittens', while the adult was known as a 'coney'. Rabbit burrows were called 'coney garths'.

Rabbits gradually came to be semi-domesticated animals. Areas of land were put aside to allow them to

Wild rabbits live in large communities in complex series of burrows, but spend much of their time above ground

breed. The offspring provided a source of meat, especially during the winter, for the Lord of the Manor. This area of land was called a warren and the keeper of the warren was called a warrener. This is the origin of the surnames Warren and Warrener.

Rabbits were first tamed and selectively bred in the monasteries and have been kept as pets since the 19th century. Emigrants took them to Australia, where they escaped and became serious agricultural pests. Even though rabbits have a long association with man the 'fancy' or pet breeds, of which there are more than 60, were developed only after the late 1890s.

Rabbits are popular pets, being responsive and very easily tamed. They are ideal pets for the older child, who can take on the responsibility for their daily needs. However, most rabbits are so good-natured that they will also tolerate mishandling by younger children.

In the past, experts believed that rabbits were closely related to rodents (rats and mice), because their large front incisor teeth continue to grow throughout their life. Recent research has shown that rabbits are more closely related to cattle, sheep and goats. This surprising finding is supported by detailed study of their teeth and body fluids.

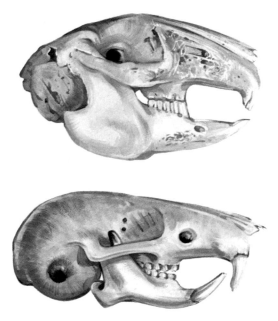

Although rabbits' teeth grow constantly and they have long, sharp front incisors, they are not rodents. A rabbit's skull (above) has significant differences from a rodent's (below)

The rodent has only two pairs of incisors compared with the rabbit's three. If you look inside a rabbit's mouth you will find, behind the upper incisors, an extra pair of small incisor teeth. Also the strange habit which rabbits have of eating the special droppings produced at night, has a similar function to cows chewing the cud.

Rabbits are sometimes confused with hares. Unlike rabbits, hares have long hind legs; their ears are longer and they do not burrow in the ground. Young hares are born covered in fur with their eyes open, while new-born rabbit kittens are hairless and blind. This confusion is easy to understand when one breed of rabbit has been named the Belgian Hare, because of a superficial resemblance to the true hare.

Choosing and buying

Rabbits are almost always family pets and it may be important to choose a breed of a size that a child can manage. Dwarf rabbits weight about 1 kg (2 lb) and a young child can handle them easily, but a Flemish Giant, weighing 5.5–10 kg (12–22 lb), requires the help of an adult. Most cross-bred petshop rabbits weigh about 2–3 kg (4–7 lb).

There are more than 60 recognized breeds of rabbit, with often more than 20 colour variations within a breed. Pure-bred rabbits are divided into the 'fancy' breeds, for example Angora, Belgian Hare, Dutch, English, Harlequin and Lops; and the 'fur' breeds, such as the

Rabbits vary considerably in size: a New Zealand White adult is far bigger than a Chinchilla Netherland Dwarf, for instance

Californian, Chinchilla and Rex. When purchasing a pure-bred you are buying a rabbit of a known adult size. Many petshop rabbits are crossbreeds, so without seeing the parents it may prove very difficult to estimate how large they will grow.

You can buy rabbits from a number of sources: a friend whose rabbit has had a litter, a breeder who specializes in pure-bred rabbits or a petshop. Whatever the source, the rabbit you purchase should be between six and eight weeks of age. Always examine the rabbit thoroughly before purchase.

Look carefully at the rabbits in the pen before handling. They should move freely and breathing should be regular and unforced, at a rate of about 40–60 breaths per minute. Even when the animal is resting, a rabbit's ears are usually pricked and it is watchful. Any droppings in the pen should be dry, well-formed brown pellets.

Pick up your chosen rabbit and stroke it gently. If you can easily feel the spine and ribs, the rabbit is thin and should not be purchased, no matter how attractive it may seem. If the animal is of a reasonable size and in good condition, check the points in the following list.

Signs of health

Nose Free from discharge with no obvious scabs. In a healthy rabbit the nose will be seen to be twitching rhythmically. Do not be tempted to buy a rabbit with a runny nose – this is a sign of the rabbit cold, often called 'snuffles' (see section on Health and ailments). It is very difficult to treat and spreads rapidly to other rabbits, so do not buy any animals from this source.

Eyes Clean and bright, not watery; no mattery discharge or puffiness around the eye. Dull eyes are usually a sign of ill health, although they can also be seen in healthy but old individuals.

Teeth Clean, correct length and growing parallel. With the mouth closed, the upper incisors should lie slightly in front of the lower teeth. If they do not meet correctly the teeth will not wear evenly and will be a constant source of trouble. Do not buy any rabbits from a litter that is so affected as this condition is inherited.

Ears Clean, no waxy discharge or encrustations. These signs are indicative of canker, a parasitic infestation of the ears. As the condition is contagious, do not buy any rabbits, even if their ears appear clean, from a source where other rabbits have these symptoms.

Skin Clean, free from scurf and cyst-like swellings, supple with no areas of redness or itchiness.

Coat Clean, sleek and shiny; look for parasites and bare patches. Take special care in examining the underside of the hock. This area is often hairless and any bare skin should be clean, but in Rex rabbits this area should always be hairy.

Limbs Claws evenly worn and short. Each leg should be checked for sores and swellings. Pay particular attention to the inside of each foreleg at wrist level: check to see if it is damp and discoloured. A rabbit with 'snuffles' will wipe its nose on this area of the foreleg which is known as the 'rabbit's handkerchief'. It is important to check this area because the animal may be so efficient at keeping its nose clean that a case of 'snuffles' may be missed.

Anus The anus should be clean and unstained; any soiling in the area is suggestive of diarrhoea.

Other pets

Rabbits prefer to be kept with company. Some people have suggested guinea pigs, others tortoises, but of course the most obvious is another rabbit. If two bucks are kept together they will fight, although not if they are castrated. Castration is a relatively simple operation which has to be done under general anaesthetic when the rabbit is about six months old. This operation may also prove its value if the male rabbit comes to be kept together with a female later on, and breeding is not desired. Few problems arise when two females are kept together.

Rabbits can live up to 12 years, but this is unusual; most rabbits show signs of senility at five or six years of age. Many of the longer-lived individuals tend to be unmated females.

Breeds

This section describes a selection of 19 more popular rabbit breeds, and concludes with a chart giving details of the weight and colour of 38 breeds. Rarer and lesser known breeds are omitted, the total recognized currently being over 60.

Large breeds

Argenté This can come in four colours: *champagne*, *bleu*, *crême* and *brun*. The Argenté rabbits originated in France, probably in the province of Champagne. They are a large meat breed and have an average litter size of about five.

Belgian Hare This is an attempt by breeders to imitate the characteristics of the wild hare. Indeed it so resembles

A cross-bred rabbit such as this one is a sturdy, less expensive and widely available alternative to a pure-bred pet rabbit

A blue Beveren, the best known of the four colour variations of the breed

a hare in both shape and size that it is difficult to believe that it is a rabbit. However, it is, and it makes an excellent pet. It is a rich chestnut colour with bold hazel eyes. For showing, individuals are trained to stand in an alert (ready to run) position.

Beveren Four colorations are available, the oldest of which, and indeed the most popular, is blue. The other colours are black, white and brown. The Beveren gets its name from its town of origin which is near Antwerp. The breed was first recognized in the 1890s and was probably introduced into the UK during the First World War. The coat is dense, silky and lustrous.

British Giant This is the largest of the British breeds of rabbit. There are many different combinations of coat and eye colours.

Californian Although this rabbit is bred mainly for meat it is very docile and makes an excellent pet for the older child. The coat is white with black or chocolate-coloured

A German giant rabbit

patches on the nose, ears, feet and tail. The markings are very similar to those on a Siamese cat.

Chinchilla Giganta This is a large strain of the Chinchilla, having a very similar coat (see Chinchilla).

Flemish Giant This is the largest of the domestic breeds of rabbit normally bred in Britain for meat. There are three main strains of Flemish: the British Flemish, which has a white belly, and the American and Dutch Flemish, which have a steel-grey belly. All strains have a steel-grey coat flecked with black. Its temperament makes it an ideal pet, but its size poses difficulties, both in hutch design and handling.

Lop The lop-eared rabbit is the oldest of the fancy breeds, with ears measuring up to 70 cm (28 in). The ears appear

Top to bottom: *a Belgium Hare, an English rabbit, an English Lop and a Dutch rabbit*

to be normal until the rabbit is about 14 days old when they begin to droop. The English Lop has much larger ears than the French Lop. A full range of colours has been bred although the most common are black, fawn or a mixture of the two.

New Zealand White Usually bred for meat or the fur trade, this docile breed also makes suitable pets. However, again because of their large size they can pose handling problems for younger children. They have a dense white

A family of French Lops

coat and pink eyes, and are therefore described as albinos.

Medium-sized breeds

Angora This is a wool-producing rabbit. The coat needs daily attention, so it is not a beginner's rabbit. The albino form is the most common, although other colours are available which have specific names:

    Agouti = Brown-grey
    Black = Smoke
    Blue   = Blue smoke
    Yellow = Golden

Chinchilla This is the most popular of the fur breeds with the coat resembling that of the true chinchilla, which is not a rabbit but a South American rodent (*Chinchilla laniger*). The fur is a deep slate in colour overlaid with bands of pearl white and tipped with black; it is particularly soft and fine. It is an extremely attractive rabbit and makes an excellent pet.

English This breed has evolved from the 'Old English'. This popular breed is white with a coloured nose, ears, eyes and chains of spots on the flanks.

Harlequin This is a long-eared rabbit with attractive and unusual markings reminiscent of a chess board. The most popular colouring is black and orange, although it is possible to obtain brown and orange, blue and cream and lilac and cream. When the orange portion of the pattern is replaced by white the variety is called a Magpie.

Rex In 1927 a rabbit with a completely new coat type was imported into Britain from France – the Rex. The coat is soft and velvet-like with no long guard hairs. Over the years breeders have selected for a plush, even coat, of which there are now over 30 different coat and eye

A particularly striking Harlequin rabbit

Left: *an Orange Rex rabbit* **Above:** *Rex and Siberian crosses*

colours and patterns. Nearly all possible colour combinations are available. Some of the colours have been given specific names, for instance:

Agouti = Castor
Albino = Ermine
Silver = Silver seal
Havana = Nutria

There is also a long-haired variety of Rex, the Opposum Rex; the only colour regularly seen was black, and this variety is now rare.

Small breeds

Dutch This is a very popular show breed but also makes an excellent pet. The coat is smooth and shiny, lying close to the body. The basic colour scheme is white combined with one other colour. There is usually a white blaze on the shoulders with a coloured abdomen, ears, cheeks and eye patches. The most popular 'other' colours are black, blue, orange-yellow, tortoiseshell and steel grey.

Himalayan This is a very attractive patterned rabbit with the same colour points as a Siamese cat. The main colour is white with the nose, ears, tail and feet coloured black,

Light Silver and Dark Blue Netherland rabbits

blue, lilac or chocolate. The young are all white until they leave the nest, when the colours start to develop.

Lop (Dwarf Lop) This rabbit has the same features as the English Lop although it is only a quarter of the weight.

Netherland Dwarf This delightful little rabbit is one of the most popular of the modern breeds and undoubtedly makes the best pet for the small child. Even when fully grown, it will sit in the palm of your hand. Two points to look for are small ears, less than 5 cm (2 in), and large, bright eyes. There are more than 30 different colours.

Polish The Polish is almost identical to the Netherland Dwarf. It was developed as a breed in the UK over many years. Until the Netherland Dwarf was imported during the 1950s only two varieties were recognized. Since then the number of colours available has increased until it rivals the Netherland. The Polish is more hare-like, with slightly longer ears and limbs.

Colour and weight chart for selected breeds

BREED	COLOUR	WEIGHT	
		kg	lb
Large			
Alaska	black	3.5–4	7.75–9.00
Argenté	four colours	3.5	8.00
Beaver	brown	4.1	9.00
Beveren	four colours	3.5–4.5	7.75–10.00
Belgian Hare	chestnut	3.5–4.0	7.75–9.00
Blanc de Bouscat	albino	6.4–6.8	14.00–15.00
Blanc de Hoto	albino	4.0–4.5	9.00–10.00
Blanc de Termonde	white	4.5–5.6	10.00–12.00
British Giant	various	5.5–7.0	12.00–15.00
Californian	white, points	3.5–5.0	7.75–11.00
Chinchilla Giganta	light grey	4.0–5.5	9.00–12.00
Flemish Giant	grey, flecks	5.5–10.0	12.00–22.00
Lop, English	full range	6.5–9.0	14.00–20.00
Lop, French	full range	4.0–5.5	9.00–12.00
New Zealand Red	red/orange	3.6	8.00
New Zealand White	albino	4.0–5.0	9.00–11.00
Rhineländer	white, patch	3.8–4.5	8.50–10.00
Thüringer	tortoiseshell	3.5–4.5	7.75–10.00
Medium			
Angora	full range	2.5–2.7	5.50–6.00
Argenté	silvered	2.5–2.8	5.50–6.20
Astrex	full range	2.7–3.6	6.00–8.00
Chinchilla	light grey	2.7	6.00
English	white, spots	2.5–3.5	5.50–7.75
Fox	white belly	2.5–3.25	5.50–7.20
Havana	chocolate	2.5–3.0	5.50–6.60
Harlequin	chequered	2.7–3.6	6.00–8.00
Rex	full range	2.5–3.6	5.50–8.00
Sable	sepia	2.4–3.3	5.30–7.30
Satin	full range	2.7–3.6	6.00–8.00
Siberian	full range	2.4–3.3	5.30–7.30
Silver	silvered	2.3–2.7	5.00–6.00
Smoke Pearl	two patterns	2.3–3.2	5.00–7.00
Small			
Dutch	various	2.0–2.5	4.50–5.50
Himalayan	colour point	2.0–2.25	4.50–5.50
Lop, Dwarf	full range	2.0	4.50
Netherland Dwarf	full range	0.9	2.00
Polish	full range	1.0	2.25
Tan	tan belly	2.0	4.50

Housing

Rabbits are traditionally housed in hutches. A well-built, roomy, draught-proof and dry hutch is basic to a rabbit's welfare. The hutch design will differ depending on whether the rabbit is to be kept indoors or outside. The basic hutch is a cage sub-divided into two interconnecting compartments. One section is fitted with a wire mesh door of 2 cm ($\frac{3}{4}$ in) chicken wire, the other is fitted with a solidly built wooden door to enable the rabbit to shelter from the elements, and to sleep undisturbed at night.

The size of the hutch depends on the adult size of the rabbits to be accommodated. For a medium-sized rabbit, a hutch 120 cm × 60 cm × 60 cm (48 in × 24 in × 24 in) or for a dwarf breed 65 cm × 65 cm × 50 cm (26 in × 26 in × 20 in) will be sufficient so that it can be used for a doe and litter. Hutches are usually made of wood.

Minimum requirements

The hutch must be raised a minimum of 23 cm (9 in) from the ground to allow free circulation of air around the cage and to give protection from rising damp, frost and predators. Raising the hutch to table top height will make cleaning, handling and feeding much easier.

Waterproofing and sealing If rabbits are housed indoors the hutch need not be as substantial as one that is to be sited outside. Although the hutch does not need to be weatherproof, its base should still be waterproofed. Many owners achieve this with a thick coat or two of gloss paint, varnish or wood preservative. The most effective treatment, however, is to apply an epoxy resin to the floor of the cage and for a distance of 2.5 cm (1 in) up the walls.

Special care should be taken to ensure that the joints between walls and floor are sealed. This will provide a hard wearing, easily cleaned surface.

Location of the hutch If the rabbit is to be housed in the garage, it should not share this accommodation with the family car, because rabbits are very susceptible to exhaust

Tiered hutches are useful for keeping numbers of rabbits on a limited floor area

fumes. In any case, the shed or garage used to house the rabbit must be well ventilated without being draughty.

For an outdoor hutch, the choice of site is important. It should be in a sheltered site facing south or south-east in order to catch the sun. During the winter it may be helpful to make thick curtains, for instance from plastic fertilizer sacks, and fix these in front of the mesh to reduce draughts. In a severe winter you must be prepared to bring all hutches indoors or at least under cover.

An outdoor hutch must have a sloping roof to throw off the rain. There should be a height difference of at least 2.5 cm (1 in) between the front and back of the roof to produce a suitable pitch. If the roof projects 15 cm (6 in) or more beyond the front of the hutch it will give added protection. The roof should be covered in roofing felt to ensure that it is waterproof.

Making a hutch

Ready-made hutches can be bought at most pet shops, but it will be cheaper to make your own. Draw the design of the hutch before embarking on the project, which will help you assess your requirements. Use 5 × 2.5 cm (2 × 1 in) wood for the frame and paint with a minimum of three coats of gloss paint, varnish or wood preservative before fixing the floor and cladding. Plywood has often been recommended as a flooring, with tongue and groove boards as a cladding. Indeed, as long as it is suitably sealed, plywood can be used for the whole construction other than the frame.

Doors Take great care in making the doors: this can save a lot of frustration. Avoid excessively large doors as they are difficult to close quickly, to prevent a rabbit's escape. However, adequate access to the interior of the hutch is essential for cleaning.

To allow ease of access it is preferable to hinge the

A hutch should have a dark section the rabbit can retreat into for privacy or rest plus a living compartment

doors on the bottom edge rather than the side. This also makes it easier to close the door after putting the rabbit back into the hutch. If the open door can be held horizontal, perhaps by attaching a chain, you can use it as a shelf when cleaning the interior. To avoid having to compromise on door sizes, you can make a removable roof.

Finishing touches Another useful idea is to place a removable board, about 5 cm (2 in) high, across the front of the hutch, as this will retain bedding and prevent it from falling out through the wire mesh or the door. You will need to be able to remove the board, however, to clean out the hutch. Because of the rabbit's known habit of gnawing, parts of the woodwork of the hutch need to be protected: metal angled edging, available from DIY shops, has proved most successful. The edging should be attached to the inner surface wherever there are exposed edges.

Day-to-day care

Preparing the floor of a hutch for a rabbit to occupy is known as 'bedding up'. Place a layer of four or five sheets of newspaper on the floor of the hutch and cover these with a mixture of sawdust and woodshavings to a depth of 5 cm (2 in). Clean, dry straw, or preferably hay, make good bedding in the sleeping quarters. In the living quarters, place a stout, bark-covered branch for the rabbit to gnaw. Gnawing is important to prevent the excessive growth of the rabbit's incisor teeth.

Cleaning out

The hutch must be cleaned out every other day. The bedding in the sleeping quarters must be changed weekly. Use a short-handled shovel or an onion hoe to remove the sawdust directly into a large bucket or bin. The rabbit will usually only soil one corner of the cage, which makes cleaning a lot easier.

At least weekly during the summer, and less frequently during the winter, scrub out the hutch with a mild disinfectant solution to control the population of flies. Rinse the hutch with clean, warm water; ensure that the hutch has dried out before you return the rabbit to it.

Replace the newspaper, sawdust and woodshavings with fresh supplies, but retain some clean portions of the old bedding to mix with fresh straw or hay in the sleeping

Frequent cleaning out of the hutch is very important

quarters. The old bedding is used to ensure that the rabbit returns to a familiar smell.

Some rabbits may become vicious if they are not removed from the hutch during cleaning. This is particularly common with a doe and litter.

Hygienic feeding and drinking

The food bowl For pelleted food or cereal mixes, you need to provide a bowl, and a heavy earthenware dog's water bowl is the most suitable. This type of bowl is difficult for the rabbit to tip over. If the bowl is tipped over the food will be trampled and soiled, and this can cause the rabbit to refuse food. It may even pick up an infection from the contaminated food.

Store food in sealable plastic containers and buy only sufficient food to last one week, to prevent it from becoming stale before use.

The drinking bottle Some people use a dog bowl to hold the rabbit's supply of drinking water, but this tends to become contaminated with bedding and faeces. Instead, animal drinking bottles, fixed outside the cage, are the most suitable. The best types are plastic bottles with a stainless steel sleeve on the end of the drinking tube. There is a tendency for these drinkers to drip excessively, but this is less likely if there are two, rather than one, stainless steel balls in the sleeve.

Paint the outside of the water bottle black to prevent algal growth, but if you do this you must leave a strip unpainted so that you can always check the water level. A strip of sellotape stuck to the side of the bottle, while it is being painted, will reveal a paint-free strip when it is pulled away.

Exercise

A rabbit needs plenty of exercise and access to a garden is immensely important for its well-being. For this you will need to ensure that all escape routes are blocked, and you may not have to mind some nibbling at your prize plants, so this requires some thought. If free access to the garden is unrealistic, consider building a pen. The problem is to make this escape-proof despite the burrowing habits of the rabbit. It will certainly be easier to start with existing walls wherever you can, and wire netting with 2–2.5 cm ($\frac{3}{4}$–1 in) mesh is suitable for the main portion of the fence. The netting will have to be buried in the ground to a minimum of 30–45 cm (12–18 in) to thwart tunnelling, and the fence should stand at least 1 m (40 in) above ground.

Morant hutches If an area of lawn is available, you can avoid all this work by using a Morant hutch. A rectangular or triangular wooden frame is covered and floored with wire-netting, with one end boxed in and floored with wood. A convenient size for such a hutch is 2 m × 1 m × 1 m (80 in × 40 in × 40 in). The wire floor allows the rabbit to graze without being able to burrow to freedom. This type of hutch must have large doors for easy access to catch the rabbit. The hutch can easily be moved as the grass is eaten, and a rabbit could spend the spring, summer and early autumn in it. Morant hutches are unsuitable for winter housing.

A triangular version of the Morant hutch

Handling
and grooming

Handling

When approaching the hutch always do so quietly to prevent panic. Talk in a calm voice as you go. The rabbit will learn to recognize your voice and respond to it. Handle the rabbit frequently and it will soon become tame.

Lifting There is only one correct way to lift a rabbit: hold the scruff of the neck with one hand and support the hind

To carry a rabbit support it from beneath and hold it steady by the scruff of its neck

quarters with the other. If a rabbit is incorrectly handled it will kick with its powerful hind legs, or bite. Beware of its sharp claws. If a rabbit starts to squeal while you are handling it, gently release it and stroke it until it calms down. This could prevent sudden death from heart failure.

Carrying It is easy to carry a rabbit: allow it to lie along your forearm, with its head snuggled into the crook of your arm. This keeps it calm while supporting its weight. To carry a young rabbit, simply support it on the palm of your hand.

Handling should start when the kitten is about seven or eight weeks of age. If a young rabbit is stroked and spoken to in a soft voice, from an early age, it is unlikely to

Baby rabbits should be handled from an early age to accustom them to human contact

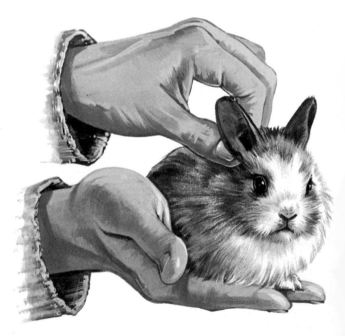

be vicious when it gets older. Take care when lifting a rabbit from a hutch, especially if the door is at shoulder height. Always return a rabbit to the hutch hind feet first, to prevent it from kicking with its strong back legs.

A rabbit must never be picked up by the ears. You can steady it by gently holding the base of the ears and its rear end

Grooming

Except for the Angora, it is not strictly necessary to groom rabbits. A healthy rabbit grooms itself, and provided its living quarters are adequately maintained, its coat will have a natural bloom.

Regular grooming does, however, give the owner the opportunity to examine the rabbit closely for signs of

Special brushes and combs are needed to keep a long-haired Angora rabbit's coat clean and untangled

disease. A table with a non-slip surface, such as sacking, makes an ideal grooming table. Grooming brushes and combs specifically designed for small animals can be readily purchased from your pet shop. Rabbits moult heavily in autumn, and then daily grooming helps to remove their loose hair.

The Angora rabbit, however, with a coat growing up to 12.5 cm (5 in) in length, needs a lot of attention. The best type of brush to use has wire bristles set in a rubber cushion. Brush with downward strokes, starting at the shoulders, until all debris in the coat is removed.

As long as the rabbit has suitable accommodation it will soil only one corner of the hutch, so soiling of the fur is unlikely to be a problem.

The glamorous Angora's fur needs frequent, thorough grooming

Food and drink

Rabbits are herbivores: they eat only vegetable matter. Their vegetarian diet needs to be a varied and balanced one, and they must be fed at regular intervals, namely two or three times a day. Three different types of food combine to make up a balanced diet: dry foods, roughage and fresh foods.

Dry foods

Pelleted food, or a rabbit mix containing oats, maize and other cereals, are the staple of the rabbit's diet. You can make your own mixture rather than purchasing it from the pet shop. It is made up as follows:

　　1 part bran
　　1 part fish meal or soya flour
　　1 part linseed cake
　　3 parts ground oats (porridge)
　　4 parts maize meal

Take enough of this mixture to provide rations for a week, and stir in a little hot water, binding it to produce a crumbly consistency. Whatever the form of dry food, do not be tempted to buy more than one month's supply, otherwise it will deteriorate before you can use it.

You can mix your own feed for a pet rabbit or buy proprietary food, according to preference and convenience

Hay, dried pelleted food and fresh fruit and vegetables are all suitable foods for rabbits

Rabbits will also take stale bread or wholemeal bread, and some experts claim that bread is good for rabbits' teeth.

Only provide enough food for one day. This prevents food being spilt or trampled, which leads to waste. Feed about one cupful (140–170 g / 5–6 oz) of dried food per day. The ideal way is to split this into two or three small meals, administered at regular times.

Roughage

The roughage portion of the ration is very important in preventing a disease known as mucoid enteritis. What do we mean by roughage? The most common forms of roughage in animal diets are hay and straw. Hay should be available to the rabbit throughout the day, but never put in more than one day's supply (85 g / 3 oz) because the rabbit will simply trample on the excess and soil it.

Never feed dusty or poor quality hay, for this can lead to respiratory and digestive upsets. If the hutch is large enough, place the hay in a rack on the wall.

Fresh foods

These are known as greens. A medium-sized rabbit will eat about 170 g (6 oz) of greens daily. Beware though, for rabbits fed exclusively on greens will develop digestive problems. Wild rabbits eat large amounts of grass, so it is perfectly safe to offer freshly-pulled bundles of grass, so long as the grass has not been treated with a weed killer. Grass cuttings, however, are bad for rabbits: they ferment too readily in a rabbit's intestine, and this causes colic.

Wild plants A variety of wild plants from the countryside will make additional nourishment for your rabbit, but do not collect these from beside roads because here they will be contaminated with lead from car exhaust fumes. Rabbits accept and avidly eat chickweed, comfrey, dandelion, docks, groundsel, plantain, sow thistles and vetches. All plants collected from the wild must be well washed before feeding to the rabbit. If you cannot positively identify a plant do not feed it to your pet, as it may be poisonous. Some plants are definitely poisonous, and these include buttercups, foxgloves, speedwell, woody nightshade, bindweed, geraniums, bluebells, black and white bryony, elder and ragwort.

Fruit and vegetables A variety of vegetables are suitable as food for rabbits, including runner and french beans (leaves and pods), purple or white sprouting broccoli (a good winter feed), cabbage (split the larger stalks before feeding), spinach and lettuce. Fruit is suitable as a titbit, and rabbits will eat prunings from fruit trees in substantial quantities. All green food should be well washed and shaken dry before feeding, to prevent leaves soiled by wild rabbits from passing any disease to your pet.

Root vegetables suitable for winter feeding include potato peelings, cooked potato mashed up with an equal amount of bran, and raw turnips cut into chips. Green raw potato must never be fed to rabbits as it contains a poison called solanine. Although clover is a very nutritious food and an excellent source of protein, take

Wild plants such as (left to right) thistles, mare's tail, dock, ribwort plantain, clover and dandelion provide free rabbit food. They must be well washed and free from sprays and car exhaust contamination

care when feeding this to rabbits as too much clover can cause a digestive upset known as 'bloat'.

Water

Fresh water must always be available to the rabbit, especially during hot weather. It is particularly important to provide extra water for does with litters, topping up the drinker three times a day.

Change the rabbits' water completely every day. Green algae, growing on the inside of water bottles, can be a nuisance. To prevent this, wash out the bottle and pipe regularly in a dilute solution of bleach. Remember to rinse everything clean before refilling with water for the rabbit. Some people use boiling water to rinse out the bottle, but this is impractical with plastic bottles.

You can exclude algae almost completely by painting the outside of the bottle black, which prevents light from stimulating their growth. The method is described in the section on Day-to-day care.

When the rabbits are eating substantial amounts of

greens they tend to drink very little water: this is quite normal.

How rabbits digest

Rabbits digest a large portion of the vegetable matter in their food in an enlarged sac-like organ at the junction of the small and large bowel called the caecum. Nutrients released by the digestion in the caecum are not immediately available to the rabbit, and can only be absorbed after the faeces have been eaten. Therefore the food passes twice through the rabbit's digestive tract: special droppings are produced at night which are dark green, soft and shiny. The rabbit picks these pellets from the vent as they are passed and eats them. Rabbits' normal droppings are quite different, being brown in colour, dry, well-formed and hard.

Rabbits with little access to a garden or run for exercise can rapidly become overweight. They deposit large quantities of fat under the skin and a dewlap may become evident, giving the appearance of a double chin. The only treatment is a combination of exercise and dieting: reduce the amount of food, while increasing the proportion of greenstuffs and bran in the diet, at the expense of pellets and corn.

Breeding and pregnancy

Breeding

Eventually many rabbit owners feel they would like to breed at least one litter. Rabbits breed most readily during the spring and early summer; this coincides with the warmer weather, which encourages survival and growth of the young and also provides a plentiful supply of green food.

Male or female? Sexing of young rabbits is often very difficult, although it is said to be easier when they are three to five days old. The kitten is turned on to its back in the palm of your hand and the genitalia are examined. The female has a short slit-shaped opening very close to the anus, whereas the male has a pointed, protruding genital opening some distance from the anus. Gentle pressure either side of this opening will cause the penis to protrude in adult males.

The best way to stop a rabbit struggling while determining its sex

To examine the genitalia of the adults, careful handling is required. With the rabbit facing away from you, hold it by the scruff of the neck with your right hand. It is then lifted by bringing your left hand under its rump from behind.

Having reached this stage you should sit down and rest the hind quarters on the upper part of your leg with its head towards you. The thumb and first finger of your left hand are then used to expose the genital openings and to apply gentle pressure to see if a penis is protruded.

Sexual maturity in rabbits varies from five months in some dwarf breeds to eight months in the giant breeds. The average pet shop rabbits can usually be bred from six to eight months of age. To prevent any unwanted pregnancies, sexes should be segregrated from the age of five months.

Mating The female (doe) is always taken to the male (buck) for mating. This is to avoid the doe attacking the buck. If the buck is placed in the doe's hutch it is likely that she will resent his intrusion and will savage him before he can be removed. When the doe is ready to mate she will lie in the correct position with her rump raised. Mating occurs very quickly and finishes with the buck falling on his side and making a muted squeak.

Gently part the fur around the rabbit's genitalia, which are slit-like in the female and round in the male

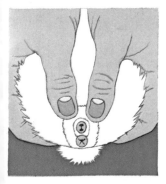 

female   male

The doe presents her rear to a buck when she is ready to mate and he mounts her. Mating between rabbits is fairly fleeting

If mating does not occur soon after the introduction, remove the doe to prevent any possible fighting. Reintroduce her daily until mating takes place, or try another buck. After mating, return the doe to her hutch. Sometimes a doe can be difficult to bring into season and one way of overcoming this is to leave her, for several days, in an uncleaned hutch that has previously housed a buck.

Pregnancy

Pregnancy lasts 30–32 days, although it is difficult to determine if the doe is pregnant until quite near delivery. During this time she should be housed in isolation from the other rabbits. She will require little special attention for the first two weeks of pregnancy, but from the 14th day onwards gradually increase the amount of food so that by the time she gives birth she will be eating twice her normal rations.

Nesting box During the third week of pregnancy, place a nesting box in the hutch plus ample supplies of good quality hay for nesting material (straw should not be used as it is too coarse). The nest box can be a specially made wooden box, measuring 25 cm × 30 cm × 40 cm (10 in × 12 in × 16 in) for the normal pet shop rabbit, or a similarly sized cardboard box.

Nest building usually takes place from the 25th day onwards. If the doe starts to build her nest on the hutch floor, rather than in the nest box, just lift it up and place it in the box provided. Most does will accept this move without resentment.

A few days before giving birth, the doe will pluck fur from her abdomen to line the nest. She will often lose her appetite at about this time: this is normal. Handle the doe as little as possible during pregnancy, and try to avoid any unnecessary disturbances, such as barking dogs or marauding cats.

The new litter Rabbits produce litters of one to 13 babies (kittens). Dwarf breeds tend to have smaller litters, while medium-sized rabbits have an average of six. Do not interfere with the nest after the doe has given birth for at least four to five days, before enticing the doe off the nest with some food. You can then examine the kittens and remove any dead or deformed ones.

To prevent the doe rejecting or attacking the kittens when she is returned, you should handle the kittens only after you have soiled your hands with the bedding in the hutch: this will disguise your smell.

Kittens are born naked, blind and deaf and are completely dependent on the mother. By the tenth day their eyes will be open and fur will have grown, but they

Baby rabbits are helpless when they are born: hairless, deaf and with their eyes still sealed

do not leave the nest for at least two to three weeks.

Because of the demands of milk production, the doe will require a continued increase in her food intake, so that by seven days after giving birth she will be eating up to three times her usual amount of food. The doe will suckle the young for about six or seven weeks, when her milk will start to dry up.

Weaning Most litters can be weaned from seven to nine weeks. By this time the doe will have lost condition and be very thin, but this is quite normal. Offer the youngsters solid food from three to four weeks of age. Although the doe can be mated again soon after weaning, it is advisable to restrict her to no more than three litters per year.

Pseudo-pregnancy Not every mating leads to a true pregnancy. Some does will apparently conceive and go through all the actions, even appearing to give birth 16–18 days after mating, but no young will result.

Fostering

If you are breeding from several does at the same time, the opportunity may arise to cross-foster kittens. A doe should not be expected to rear more than six kittens in any one litter. If more than one doe has a litter at the same time, any excess kittens can be fostered on to another doe with a smaller litter.

The best time to foster kittens is within 24 hours of birth, although it can be done for up to four days after birth. The doe is removed from the hutch and the foster kittens are introduced into the nest.

The doe should be kept away from the litter for at least half an hour so that the foster kittens take on the smell of their companions. Before reintroducing the doe it is useful to apply a scent around her nose. Such scents include petroleum jelly and aftershave. Do not apply the aftershave directly to the nose, but only to the surrounding furry areas. This scent will further confuse the doe's sense of smell and make the acceptance of the foster kitten even more likely.

Hand-rearing If there is no opportunity to cross-foster, or if kittens are not accepted, it may become necessary to attempt to rear kittens by hand. Hand-rearing is, however, very difficult and seldom successful. Here is a milk formula that has been used successfully:

  1 egg yolk
  45 ml (half a cup) of evaporated milk
  45 ml (half a cup) of water
  5 ml (1 tsp) honey
  5 ml (1 tsp) ABIDEC drops

Although frequency of feeding depends to a certain extent on the size of the kittens, the newly born are fed about every 12 hours, starting with 2 ml ($\frac{1}{2}$ tsp) of the mixture, given with an eye dropper. This amount increases daily, so that by the fourth day it is as much as 15 ml or nearly 4 tsp. By the fourth day, too, frequency of feeding should drop to once a day. Rabbits would naturally feed their young only once a day, so you should avoid overfeeding.

Hold newborn kittens on their backs in a cupped hand when feeding them from the dropper, as this is the normal nursing position for newborn kittens when suckling.

If the rabbits continue to grow well, you can offer them solid food from the tenth day.

Breeding data

Gestation period	30–32 days
Litter size (average)	7
Birth weight	30–70 g
Eyes open	8–10 days
Weaning age	42–55 days
Weaning weight	300–800 g
Puberty	90–120 days
Age to breed	120–300 days
Oestrus	stimulus male
Retire from breeding	M 3–4, F 2–3 years

Baby rabbits soon develop into smaller versions of their parents

Introduction to genetics

The many pure breeds of rabbits available to the exhibitor or pet owner have been developed by breeders. To understand this development, a simple introduction to genetics is useful.

After mating, a sperm cell and an ovum fuse in the doe's uterus, initiating the development that leads to the birth of a kitten some 30 days later. In each of these germ cells is a nucleus, the home for the key to heredity, the chromosomes. Each rabbit germ cell has 22 chromosomes; this means that after fertilization the resultant egg contains 22 pairs of chromosomes, making 44 in all. Along the chromosomes are genes which control the development of certain characteristics such as eye colour, coat texture etc. In this way the kittens receive characteristics from their mother and their father.

In each pair of chromosomes, the genes coding for a particular characteristic appear in the same place. If both genes select, for instance, for a black coat, the rabbit's coat will be black. However, it happens that the black gene will dominate over the white if the two come together. Thus if one gene selects for black and one for white, the coat is still likely to be black. The picture becomes more interesting in the next generation, however, for the black-coated offspring of such a rabbit may in turn produce white offspring. Let us consider this simple example a little more.

We can represent a black gene by a capital B and a white gene by a small b. The table below shows the various combinations of these letters:

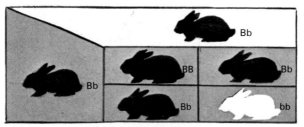

RABBITS

Any kitten with a capital B gene in the pair is black and it can be seen that three of the combinations would produce black kittens (BB, Bb, bB) and only one (bb) would produce white. Under some circumstances where neither gene is dominant, a combination of bB or Bb would produce a grey coat, the darker colour being diluted by the white.

This is a very simple introduction and it is rare to consider just one pair of genes. But if the genetic make-up of a rabbit is known the breeder will understand why the colours vary in a litter.

The genes are not fixed and occasionally they may mutate and a new expression of a characteristic will be seen. This happened in the case of the Rex and Angora breeds when the genes controlling coat type underwent mutation. Once this has happened a breeder will have to breed selectively to enhance the character, so that it is not lost. This is normally done by in-breeding, i.e. son mated with mother, or father with daughters. This type of breeding will concentrate the characteristics. However, at the same time it may be a cause of an increase in genetic diseases. To prevent this, the breeder must occasionally introduce new genes to promote 'hybrid vigour'.

An Old English rabbit and litter

Health and ailments

It is advisable to isolate a sick rabbit from its companions and to seek veterinary advice as soon as possible. A number of rabbit diseases can prove fatal without early treatment and careful nursing. Some rabbit diseases can be transmitted to man, particularly children, so follow these rules:

1 Wash your hands after handling a rabbit or cleaning out a hutch.

2 Wash the rabbit's food bowls and water bottles separately from the household crockery. Buy a washing up bowl which is used only for this purpose, and mark it so that no mistakes occur. Do not use the drainer in the kitchen for any of the rabbit's utensils. Rinse in clean water and dry with paper towels.

3 Store rabbit food separately from your own household food supplies and keep it in sealable containers to prevent access to vermin. Buy the dried food in small quantities only, so it is always in a fresh state when you feed it to the rabbit.

4 Never bring animals into or near the place food is prepared or stored.

5 Never eat, drink or smoke while playing with a rabbit or while cleaning out a hutch. Be careful to avoid doing anything that may transfer dirt from the rabbit or hutch to your lips.

6 When young children play with a rabbit or clean a hutch, an adult should supervise and ensure that the children follow these rules and that they learn the elements of hygiene.

Ailments

Overgrown claws Rabbit's claws may well need clipping once or twice a year. Take the rabbit to the vet if you are unsure how to do it. Once you have been shown how to clip the nails it is easy.

Trim your rabbit's claws a couple of times a year if they haven't worn down naturally. Don't cut into the vein, which is clearly visible

Overgrown teeth The front or incisor teeth of rabbits grow continually throughout their life. Wild rabbits keep them short by continually gnawing at branches, bark and other hard foods.

Domesticated rabbits tend to be offered much softer foods. If your rabbit lacks sufficient gnawing material, its incisor teeth will grow longer and longer and in neglected cases the animal will be unable to eat.

In some rabbits, the teeth are positioned incorrectly in the mouth and they do not work properly against an opposing tooth. This condition usually affects the molar or cheek teeth. As the condition may be inherited, affected animals should not be used for breeding.

Rabbits with teeth problems tend to have a ragged coat because of difficulties with grooming. The mouth and chin are often soaked in saliva because the animal drools uncontrollably.

A rabbit with overgrown or badly positioned teeth often becomes very thin because eating becomes difficult, and a badly neglected one may even starve to death. However, the vet will often be able to cure the problem. He or she can easily trim down overgrown teeth, and you can prevent the condition from recurring by providing the rabbit with harder foods, such as sprout and cabbage stalks, or with a gnawing block. This is made from freshly-cut branches that are still covered in bark; the best wood to use is apple.

Heat stroke This is most common in pregnant does during the summer. The affected rabbit is usually found in a collapsed state, breathing very rapidly. The rabbit should be brought in out of sun and plunged into *tepid* water. Pregnant does often abort after suffering from this condition. Always take special care to ensure that the doe has adequate shade throughout the day. If necessary, move the hutch from direct sunlight.

Mucoid enteritis This disease can affect rabbits of all ages. The main clinical sign is diarrhoea which contains mucus. Affected rabbits dehydrate rapidly and usually die unless treated. First, remove pelleted foods and corn mixes from the diet and replace these with hay for at least three days. Provide plenty of water containing salt (1 tsp in a pint). Seek veterinary treatment if the rabbit has not improved within 48 hours. If a rabbit recovers from mucoid enteritis it does not become immune, and the condition will recur unless more roughage is provided in the diet.

Myxomatosis This distressing virus disease nearly wiped out the wild rabbit population in the UK during the 1950s. It is still present in the wild population and the agent of transmission is the rabbit flea. Clinical signs include swelling of the eyelids until the rabbit is unable to open its eyes, and swelling of the nose, mouth and anus. Most infected rabbits die in spite of treatment.

You can act to prevent myxomatosis by keeping out the rabbit flea, its deadly carrier. Use flea powders on the rabbit and an environmental spray in the hutch. A vaccine is available, which comes in packs of ten doses which all have to be used at the same time. The vaccine also has to be administered every year to ensure protection.

Paralysis Rabbits can become paralysed as a result of mishandling, usually when someone lifts them up without supporting the hind end. Seek veterinary advice as soon as possible. If the rabbit loses control of its bladder and continually trickles urine, it will not recover and should be put to sleep. Animals with only partial paralysis should be closely confined for two weeks to see if they will recover. Food and water must be within easy reach at all times. To prevent 'bed sores', provide deep bedding and change it frequently.

Snuffles Infections of the respiratory tract of rabbits are very common. They produce symptoms akin to those seen with a common cold in man. Snuffles is usually seen in rabbits over three or four weeks old and the clinical signs include continual sneezing, watery discharge from nose and eyes and as the condition progresses, apathy and loss of appetite.

A rabbit with snuffles will be seen washing its face at frequent intervals, removing the discharges from the nose. The inside of the foreleg becomes wet and discoloured as a consequence. The illness can progress rapidly to a fatal pneumonia, or it may become chronic, with the discharges becoming thicker. In the chronic condition, the rabbit continues to have snuffles for months until it starts to lose weight and develop pneumonia, and then it dies.

Only treatment by a vet, in the earliest stages of the disease, is ever successful. There is no effective treatment for chronically infected rabbits.

Obesity Rabbits with no access to a garden or a run for exercise can become very over-weight. The rabbit deposits large amounts of fat under the skin and a dewlap may become evident, giving the rabbit a double chin. The only treatment is a combination of dieting and exercise. Green foods and bran should be increased in the diet, with a complementary decrease in pelleted foods and corn mixtures.

Obesity is a contributing factor in 'sore hock', a condition affecting rabbits kept in dirty conditions on rough, urine-soaked flooring. Initial treatment should consist of bathing the sore hocks in a weak salt solution. If there is little response, the rabbit should be taken to the vet. Cage hygiene must be improved and a good deep bed provided, to prevent the hocks from touching the flooring.

Coccidiosis Coccidia are microscopic parasites which infest either the liver or the lining of the intestine. The infestation is often spread from an affected doe to her kittens during the first week of life. Kittens so infected usually die during the sixth or seventh week.

Rabbits with coccidiosis are very depressed, refuse

Unlike other animals, rabbits will overfeed if given the chance and become obese. It is no kindness to give a rabbit more food than it needs

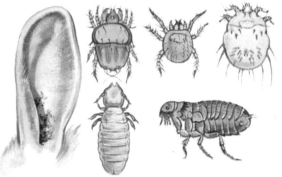

Left: *signs of ear canker;* **right** *(greatly enlarged): ticks, lice and fleas*

food, drink excessively and develop diarrhoea. If the liver is infected, the abdomen becomes very swollen and jaundice may develop. Not all infected animals will show symptoms, and those with only a light infection will become immune to the coccidia.

Veterinary treatment must be sought immediately if any rabbits are to be saved. Coccidiosis is a disease fostered by dirt; cleanliness is an excellent way to prevent it.

External parasites Fleas, ticks, lice and mites can all cause problems in rabbits. The rabbit flea can be found in the coat during grooming, but the adult fleas are usually found feeding along the edges of the rabbit's ear. Fleas transmit myxomatosis so it is vitally important to kill them. Flea powders from the pet shop should be effective: if in doubt, ask the vet.

Ticks sometimes attach themselves to rabbits, remaining for three to four days. During this period the tick feeds on the rabbit's blood and gradually increases in size. The tick embeds its mouthparts into the skin and unless the tick is removed carefully, its mouthparts will be left behind, causing sepsis. To remove a tick, cover its body in liquid paraffin or petroleum jelly, leave for 30 minutes then try to gently pull it free, using forceps. If this procedure worries you, take the rabbit to the vet.

Lice and mites both produce the same type of symptoms: itchiness, hair loss, scurf and scratching. Treatment with flea powder, both on the rabbit and in the bedding, is usually successful.

One species of mite can infest rabbits' ears, causing a condition called 'canker'. The rabbit shows obvious signs of distress and irritation, scratching at the ears and violently shaking its head. Brown, waxy encrustations will become evident in the ear as the condition progresses. If treatment with canker drops (not powder) from the pet shop does not provide rapid relief for the rabbit, ask the vet.

Mastitis Mastitis is most commonly seen when a doe's litter has to be weaned suddenly. It may happen that three to four weeks after giving birth, the doe runs out of milk, or she may become prone to attacking the kittens when they disturb her with their demands for suckling. To save the kittens, they will have to be weaned much earlier than the normal age of seven to eight weeks. A likely consequence, especially if the rabbits are not in expert care, is that the doe will sicken and develop hard lumps in her mammary glands.

If the glands are expressed, a pussy material comes out. The glands will also be hot, swollen and painful. Urgent veterinary advice is needed, as successful treatment depends on antibiotic therapy.

Abscesses These are very common in rabbits, especially around the head and shoulders. They may be caused by fighting, sharp edges or exposed wire ends in the hutch or as a complication of snuffles. Rabbit abscesses are unusual in that they rarely cause the rabbit any discomfort. They tend to build up in size under the skin and then burst, releasing a thick, sticky, white pus.

It is a waste of time bathing the abscesses, as they only refill and burst again. The only effective cure is for the abscess to be dissected free while the rabbit is under anaesthetic. If this is delayed the abscess may well spread, causing further complications.

Fly strike This is one of the most disgusting conditions seen by veterinary surgeons; nobody likes to see an animal being eaten alive by maggots which is what this problem is. It is particularly common during the summer in the older rabbit. The combination of diarrhoea and a dirty hutch often leads to flies being attracted to the hutch. The flies lay their eggs in the diarrhoea-laden fur around the rabbit's tail. The eggs hatch and the maggots eat into the flesh.

If the condition is seen early, the rabbit can be saved. Daily washing and flushing with water to remove the maggots will lead to a gradual improvement over a long period of time. This condition is caused by neglect, so even though you should be ashamed of yourself if it occurs, do not hesitate to get the rabbit to the vet.

Diseases dangerous to humans

If any of the following diseases are diagnosed by the vet, treatment will not be recommended and the affected rabbit should be put to sleep. These are called 'zoonotic diseases', which means that they can be transmitted to man.

None of these diseases is likely to be present in rabbits purchased from a clean, healthy source.

Listeriosis This disease causes abortions in pregnant does and can cause young rabbits to develop fits.

Mange Dry, scabby, itchy scales develop on the rabbit's face, belly and feet. This infestation may be associated with a similar one in the owner, which affects the hands and wrist. The rash is often so itchy that it causes scratching, which in turn leads to further infections of the skin.

Pseudo-tuberculosis Infected rabbits rapidly lose weight and develop an intractable diarrhoea. The infection in rabbits is caught by eating greens soiled by wild birds or other rabbits. It spreads to man when hands become contaminated by diarrhoea and hygiene is inadequate.

Salmonellosis Salmonella is a bacteria associated with food poisoning in man. This infection can cause abortion in pregnant does and diarrhoea.

Ringworm A fungal disease that causes circular bald patches on the head and feet. It is especially infectious to children who cuddle their pet rabbit.

A well-cared for and healthy rabbit is an appealing pet

Exhibiting

Having kept and bred rabbits successfully for a number of years, many owners start to think about showing. This is the time when visiting shows, looking at winning rabbits and talking to exhibitors will pay dividends. From contacts made at these shows you could learn of a source of good quality 'pure' breeding stock to start your strain of show rabbits.

The British Rabbit Council While exhibiting at local shows may be unrestricted (open to everyone), only registered rabbits may be exhibited in shows run under the auspices of the British Rabbit Council (BRC). If you want to exhibit seriously, you will have to register with the BRC. Registration requires the payment of an annual subscription and, when pedigree rabbits are sold, the payment of a transfer fee.

Show rings All show rabbits are identified by rings which the BRC supplies to individual breeders. These 'show rings' are slipped on to the hind leg of the rabbit, above the hock, when it is eight to 12 weeks old. As the rabbit grows, the ring can no longer be slipped over the hock and therefore permanently identifies the rabbit.

Rings are marked with the year of issue and are date-coded, so that you can easily determine the age of the rabbit. As the breeds differ in adult size, the rings vary in size, and are marked with an identification letter for the breed. Letters required for some of the common breeds are set out in the following table:

Ring letter	Breed
A	Polish
B	Dutch, Dwarf Lop, Himalayan
D	Chinchilla, English
E	Angora, Harlequin, Rex
G	Belgian Hare, English Lop
H	French Lop, New Zealand White
L	Californian
X	Netherland Dwarf

A ring above the rear hock of a show rabbit indicates its age and breed. They are put onto young rabbits and do not trouble them

Having established a show strain, many exhibitors register a prefix with the BRC. The use of prefixes allows the construction of pedigree charts so that a rabbit's ancestry can be accurately recorded.

Preparing for the show

Rabbits must be carefully prepared for exhibiting by good feeding, grooming and careful, regular handling. It is particularly important to handle show rabbits regularly every day. A rabbit which kicks, scratches and wriggles to be free will hardly impress a judge.

Rabbits younger than four months can be exhibited in special classes but they are not at their best until they are aged at least six months.

When showing a rabbit, you can enhance the natural gloss of its coat by stroking it with a clean silk handkerchief. If the coat is in poor condition because of a heavy moult, it is a waste of time showing the rabbit.

The only major item of expense is a travelling box. This can be a purpose-built wooden box, or a simple cardboard cat box. Whichever type you use, cover the floor with sawdust and some hay, and place some toasted bread in the box for the rabbit to eat. Do not give greens as the rabbit tends to trample on these and soil them, which may lead to discoloration of its coat.

There are a number of different types of show in which you can enter your rabbit:

Local club shows This type of show is often called a table show. Exhibitors sit and wait their turn, and when

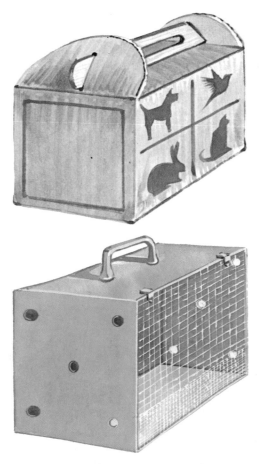

An amply sized and well-ventilated travelling box is essential for transporting your rabbits to shows, or elsewhere

their number is called they take their rabbit from the box to the judge's table where it is examined.

Pen shows Where there is a larger entry it is usual to have a 'pen show'. The rabbits are placed in individual pens and identified by a small gummed label placed inside the ear. A steward carries the rabbits to the judging table.

RABBITS

Local club and pen shows have few restrictions on entry, unlike open shows.

Open shows To enter one of these, you usually have to obtain an entry form and send it in some time before the show in order to gain acceptance. It is important to fill this in correctly so that your rabbit is placed in the correct category. Many categories are known by abbreviations and some of the more common are listed below:

Initials	Meaning
A A	Any age
A C	Any colour
Ad	Adult
AOC	Any other colour
AOV	Any other variety
ASS	Adult stock show
AV	Any variety
CC	Challenge certificate
YSS	Young stock show

Show pens for rabbit exhibiting

Useful addresses

British Rabbit Council (B R C). Purefoy House, 7 Kirkgate, Newark, Nottinghamshire NG24 1AD.

Commercial Rabbit Association (CRA FF), Tyning House, Shurdington, Cheltenham, Gloucestershire GL51 5XF.

People's Dispensary for Sick Animals (PDSA). PDSA House, Dorking, Surrey RH4 2LB.

Royal Society for the Prevention of Cruelty to Animals (RSPCA). Causeway, Horsham, East Sussex RH12 1HG.

Addresses for individual breed societies are not listed as the secretaries change annually.

Index

Photographic acknowledgments
Bruce Coleman – Jane Burton 15, 19, 20, Hans Reinhard 16, 42; Nature Photographers – S. C. Bisserot 18, E. A. Janes 22, 48; The Photo Source – Colour Library International 21, 56

Illustrations by Linden Artists Ltd (David Thompson)